0/20

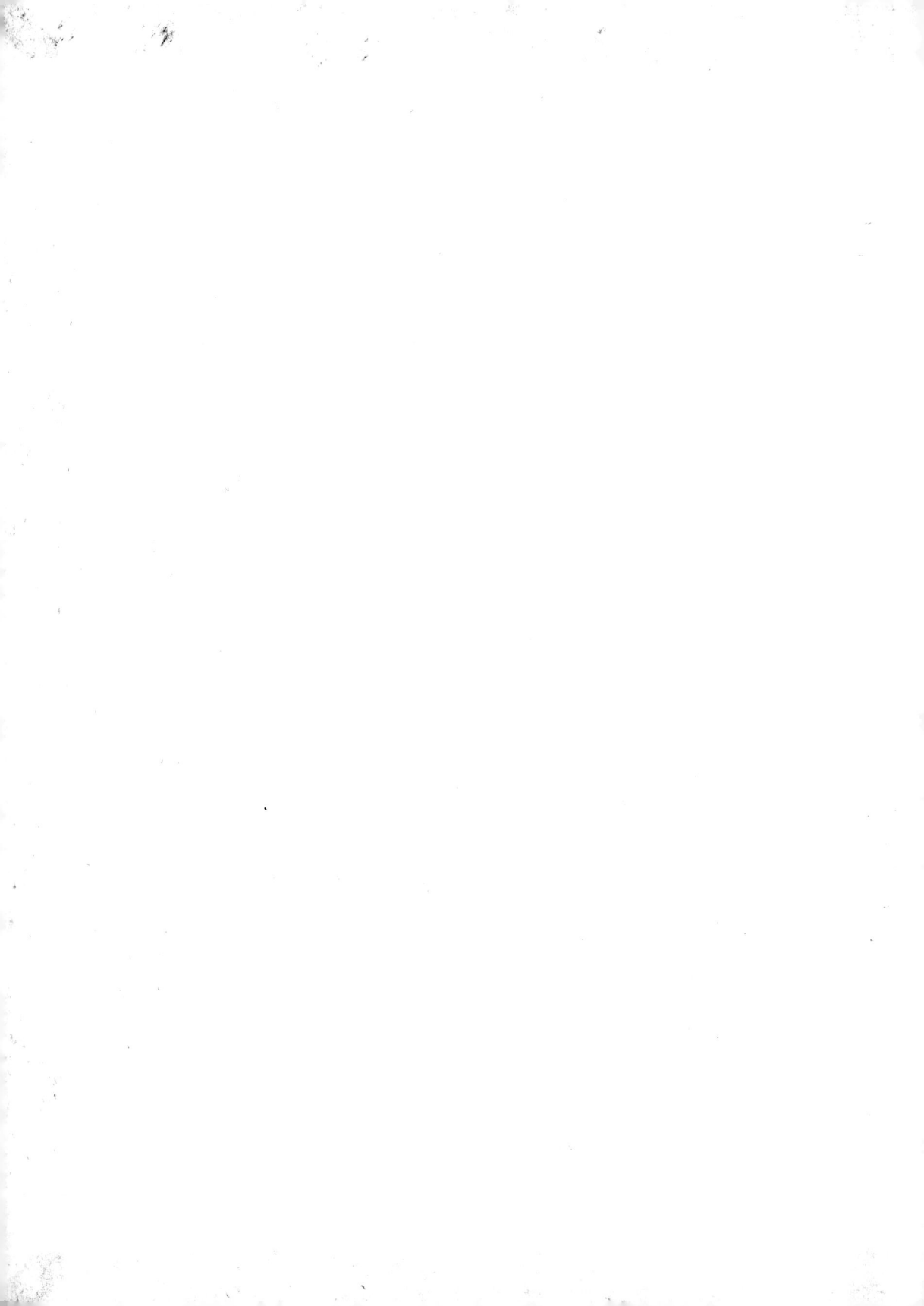

ALTERNATOR BOOKS™

MISTY COPELAND

PRINCIPAL BALLERINA

HEATHER E. SCHWARTZ

Lerner Publications ◆ Minneapolis

Lerner Publications Company
An imprint of Lerner Publishing Group, Inc.
241 First Avenue North
Minneapolis, MN 55401 USA

For reading levels and more information, look up this title at www.lernerbooks.com.

Main body text set in Aptifer Sans LT Pro.
Typeface provided by Linotype AG.

Editor: Andrea Nelson **Designer:** Lindsey Owens

Library of Congress Cataloging-in-Publication Data

The Cataloging-in-Publication Data for *Misty Copeland: Principal Ballerina* is on file
    at the Library of Congress.
ISBN 978-1-5415-9708-2 (lib. bdg.)
ISBN 978-1-72841-302-0 (pbk.)
ISBN 978-1-5415-9971-0 (eb pdf)

Manufactured in the United States of America
1-47812-48252-1/14/2020

TABLE OF CONTENTS

DANCING HER DREAM

MISTY COPELAND HAD DANCED IN *SWAN LAKE* MANY TIMES THROUGHOUT HER CAREER. But for the past fourteen years, she'd danced with the corps de ballet. Then, in April 2015, the unthinkable happened. She was cast in the lead role, set to dance the part of Odette/Odile. It was a dream come true for any ballerina. And for Copeland, it had special significance.

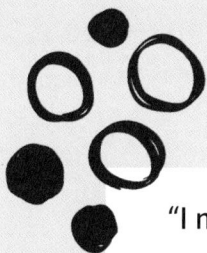

"I never imagined that I would ever have an opportunity to be Odette/Odile," she said. "I think just subconsciously when you don't see someone that looks like you represented in certain ballets, you just don't even think that it's an opportunity that you can have."

Yet there she was, making history as the first African American ballerina to dance the role with the American Ballet Theatre. Onstage at the Kennedy Center in Washington, DC, she focused her energy on a performance that would tell a story through perfectly executed movements. Offstage, she hoped her work would help advance other dancers of color working to succeed in ballet.

"The special thing about doing this in DC is that Septime Webre, Washington Ballet's artistic director, has a relationship with the Boys & Girls Clubs, which is where I took my first ballet class," she explained at the time. "This is not just a gimmick. It will speak directly to these communities and kids. A child might have more confidence to try ballet because they saw us in the media."

WESTERN AUTO

CHAPTER 1
DISCOVERING DANCE

MISTY COPELAND WAS BORN ON SEPTEMBER 10, 1982, IN KANSAS CITY, MISSOURI. When she was two, her parents, Sylvia DelaCerna and Doug Copeland, divorced, and Sylvia moved Misty and her three siblings to California. They lived in a house with an ocean view with Sylvia's new husband—Misty's stepfather—Harold Brown. Misty's half sister, Lindsey, was born during this time.

Misty was seven when she watched a movie about Nadia Comaneci, a Romanian gymnast, and fell in love with movement. She practiced gymnastics in her front yard. She also learned dance routines from her mom, who was a former cheerleader for the Kansas City Chiefs football team. Practicing gymnastics and dance felt freeing. But life at home was far from peaceful. Her mother's marriage to Brown began to break down. Soon it was over—and Misty's life changed dramatically.

Nadia Comaneci performs during the 1976 Olympic Games in Montreal, Canada.

Misty was first introduced to ballet at her local Boys & Girls Club.

"We were pretty much homeless, and we were living in a motel trying to scrape up enough money just to go to the corner store and get a cup of noodle soup to eat," she said.

But things were not all bleak. Her middle school drill team coach noticed her talent and encouraged her to take a free ballet class at the local Boys & Girls Club. Right away, the teacher, Cynthia Bradley, was impressed. She offered Misty a scholarship to her ballet school in San Pedro.

"Having someone believe in me is why I think I dove into it," she said.

Support from her teacher gave Misty the confidence to start thinking about a future in ballet. She started applying to ballet academies. But she was met with rejection letters that suggested that her body type was not right for ballet.

Misty couldn't change the body she was born with. And prejudice against her figure was not the only obstacle she faced. Her mother was working two jobs to support the family, and the two-hour commute to the dance studio only strained her further. Finally, Misty's mother told her it was too much. She wanted Misty to quit ballet.

GETTING IT DONE!

Misty started ballet years later than most female dancers do. To catch up, she practiced for hours each day and learned to dance en pointe within three months of starting her training.

CHAPTER 2

LEAPING OVER OBSTACLES

As she moved into Bradley's home, ballet became Misty's primary focus.

WHEN MISTY TOLD BRADLEY SHE HAD TO QUIT, BRADLEY OFFERED TO HOST MISTY IN HER HOME SO SHE COULD CONTINUE TRAINING. Misty took her up on the offer. In 1998, when she was fifteen, Misty won first prize in ballet at the Los Angeles Music Center Spotlight Awards. Then she won a full scholarship to train with the San Francisco Ballet School for the summer.

Bradley recognized Misty's talent and was determined to help her continue dancing.

Just as Misty was gaining attention for her talent, tensions between Misty's mother and Bradley began to grow. Misty's mother resented Bradley's influence in her daughter's life. She didn't want Misty living with her teacher anymore. Misty worried that her mother might not let her continue to dance.

GETTING IT DONE!

Misty trained for four years to get into the American Ballet Theatre. She was homeschooled for a year so she could focus on dance classes every day.

The legal battle between Misty's mother and Bradley took an emotional toll on the young dancer.

Bradley and Misty's mother went to court, battling over custody. Misty filed for emancipation so she could make her own choice about where to live. The case involving the young ballet prodigy made national headlines and daytime talk shows, which embarrassed Misty. Finally, when her mother promised she could still dance, Misty decided to move back in with her family.

After leaving Bradley's home, Misty attended San Pedro High School and studied ballet at Lauridsen Ballet Centre in Torrance, California. When she was sixteen, the American Ballet Theatre invited her to join the Studio Company. She agonized over whether to accept. Joining the company would mean leaving home to live on her own. She'd miss the birth of her niece, her high school prom, and graduation.

Trusting her gut, Misty turned them down and hoped they'd ask again. They did. After graduating from high school in 2000, she attended an American Ballet Theatre summer intensive program. She was again invited to join the Studio Company. This time, she said yes and moved to New York City.

Misty would be a member of the American Ballet Theatre for six years before becoming a soloist.

Dancer and actress Victoria Rowell (*right*) became a mentor for Copeland after her spine injury.

By eighteen, Copeland was a member of the American Ballet Theatre's corps de ballet. But a few months into her dream career, she learned she had a fracture in her spine. She had to wear a brace and stop dancing for a year. Hormones used to treat her weak bones changed her body almost overnight. She went from having the traditional figure of a ballerina—long and slender—to looking much more curvy and, eventually, muscular.

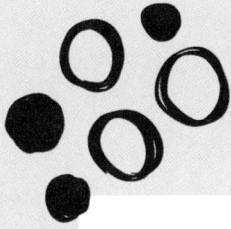

It took time for Misty to adjust to her new physique. She found a mentor in a former dancer, who helped her focus on her body's health and strength over size and appearance.

All she had to do was convince those around her that she belonged at the top level of ballet.

"DANCING HAD ALWAYS MADE ME HAPPY, AND I WANTED THAT BACK," MISTY SAID. "SO MY PRIORITY BECAME SIMPLY ACCEPTING MY NEW SELF. I FOCUSED ON WHAT I WANTED: TO FEEL GOOD, TO BE CONFIDENT IN MY SKIN AGAIN, TO DANCE."

CHAPTER 3
PROVING HERSELF

FOR THE NEXT DECADE, COPELAND WAS THE ONLY AFRICAN AMERICAN BALLERINA WITH THE AMERICAN BALLET THEATRE. She longed to become a principal dancer. But at times, she felt she would never be fully accepted as a black dancer. She could tell that when other professionals criticized her body, they were really talking about her race. Once, she was told to use makeup before a performance to lighten her skin so she would match the other dancers.

Prejudices against African American bodies meant Copeland had to prove she belonged in professional ballet.

"Dancers of color are different and not what audiences are used to seeing," she said. "The world has a view of what they think black body types are, and it doesn't fit the 'ballet' mold. They think of flat feet and big butts. . . . It's a stereotype."

GETTING IT DONE!

Copeland was the American Ballet Theatre's first African American soloist in two decades.

Copeland signs a copy of her book *Life in Motion* for a fan.

Despite the challenges she faced, Copeland's talent and drive were undeniable. In 2007 she became a soloist with the company. She impressed audiences with solos in famous ballets including *The Firebird*, *Le Corsaire*, and *Swan Lake*. Her work opened the door to other opportunities. In 2009 the late singer Prince asked her to appear in his music video for the song "Crimson and Clover." She also appeared in shows with him during his tour.

Copeland was named National Youth of the Year Ambassador for the Boys & Girls Clubs of America in 2013. She also launched Project Plié at the American

Ballet Theatre to foster diversity in dance. The following year, she published two books. *Life in Motion: An Unlikely Ballerina* tells her story to fans and future generations of dancers. The picture book *Firebird* encourages young readers to work toward their dreams. Also in 2014, she was appointed by President Barack Obama to the President's Council on Sports, Fitness and Nutrition.

Copeland unveils the Misty Copeland Barbie doll.

YOU'RE THE BOSS

From the start of her training, Misty devoted hours of time each day to ballet. Even when her dreams seemed out of reach, she never stopped working toward them.

If you have a dream or goal, devotion like Misty's can help you get there. Whether your passion is sports, music, dance, or another activity, make time each day or week to practice. No matter what your skill level when you start out, practice will help you improve.

While you're doing your thing, don't waste time worrying about whether you're good enough. And don't listen to naysayers who tell you to give up. Seek out people who support you. Most important, keep doing what you love.

Copeland was always happy to mentor young dancers. She was a role model who could show them they belonged in the world of ballet, no matter where they came from. But there was one dream she still hadn't reached herself. She wanted to be a principal with the American Ballet Theatre.

When Copeland joined the American Ballet Theatre, it had never had an African American principal dancer in its entire history.

CHAPTER 4

BLAZING THE TRAIL

Copeland poses with Raven Wilkinson (*left*), the first African American woman to dance with a major ballet company, in 2015.

ON JUNE 30, 2015, COPELAND'S MOMENT FINALLY CAME. She was the first African American woman promoted to principal dancer in the American Ballet Theatre's seventy-five-year history. Walking down the red-carpeted hallway to the dressing rooms at the Metropolitan Opera House, she knew how hard she'd worked to get there. She knew others had paved the way for her, and she could be a trailblazer for future black and brown ballet dancers.

"I had moments of doubting myself, and wanting to quit, because I didn't know that there would be a future for an African American woman to make it to this level," she said. "At the same time, it made me so hungry to push through, to carry the next generation."

Copeland (*right*) speaks to interviewer Soledad O'Brien about being a role model in the ballet community.

Soon after the announcement, Copeland made her Broadway debut with a role in the musical *On the Town*. She also continued giving back, partnering with MindLeaps, a dance program for at-risk youth in Rwanda, Guinea, and other countries.

Copeland takes a bow after a performance of the Broadway musical *On the Town.*

Copeland (*right*) poses with her husband, Olu Evans.

Copeland married her longtime boyfriend Olu Evans in 2016. She joked that when her dance career ended, her husband would have to fill the void in her life. She knew she wouldn't be able to dance forever—most ballet dancers retire in their thirties—but she'd learned a lot over the years about perseverance and taking things one day at a time.

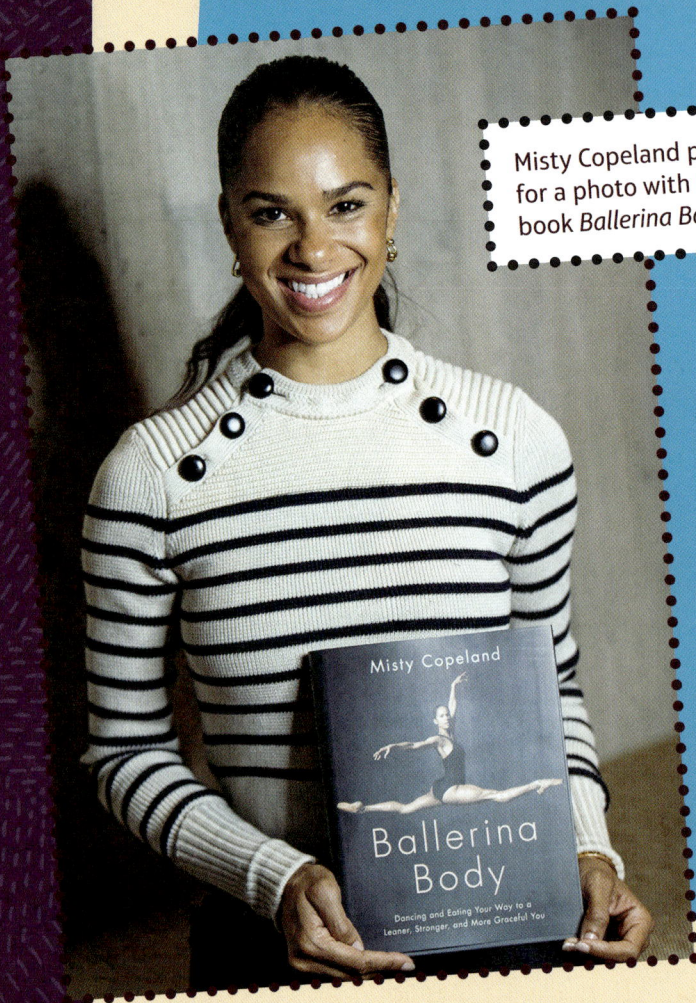

Misty Copeland poses for a photo with her book *Ballerina Body*.

Copeland published *Ballerina Body*, a book about health and strength, in 2017. In 2019 she modeled for the legendary Pirelli calendar. That year, plans were announced for a movie based on her memoir, *Life in Motion*.

Copeland still has more to look forward to and plenty of work to do.

"THE BIGGEST THING THAT I'VE LEARNED THROUGHOUT THIS JOURNEY IS TO ALLOW YOURSELF TO DREAM," COPELAND SAID. "IT'S NEVER TOO LATE. WHEN YOU PUT THE HARD WORK IN, YOU NEVER KNOW WHAT OPPORTUNITIES WILL PRESENT THEMSELVES."

Copeland continues working with the Boys & Girls Club to inspire leaders for a new generation.

TIMELINE

1982   Misty Copeland is born on September 10 in Kansas City, Missouri.

2000   She joins the American Ballet Theatre.

2007   She becomes the American Ballet Theatre's first African American soloist in twenty years.

2014   She publishes *Life in Motion: An Unlikely Ballerina*, a memoir, and *Firebird*, a picture book. She is appointed to the President's Council on Sports, Fitness and Nutrition.

2016   She marries longtime boyfriend Olu Evans.

2017   She publishes *Ballerina Body*.

2019   She models for the Pirelli calendar. Plans are announced for a movie based on her memoir, *Life in Motion*.

GLOSSARY

corps de ballet: a group of dancers who are not soloists

emancipation: to free someone from someone else's control or power

en pointe: on the tips of the toes

intensive program: several advanced dance classes and educational courses over three weeks for ballet dancers

perseverance: to continue trying to do something even though it is difficult

prejudice: unfriendly feelings directed against an individual, a group, or a race

principal: a dancer at the highest level in a professional ballet company

scholarship: an amount of money given by a school to a student to help pay for the student's education

stereotype: an often unfair and untrue belief that many people have about all people or things with a particular characteristic

SOURCE NOTES

5   "Being Odette/Odile," YouTube video, 3:56, posted by American Ballet Theatre, June 9, 2017, http://bit.ly /beingodette.

5   Candice Thompson, "10 Minutes with Misty Copeland and Brooklyn Mack," *Dance Magazine*, April 1, 2015, http://bit.ly/CopelandMack.

8   Avianne Tan, "Misty Copeland: From Kid Raised in Motel Room to Principal Ballerina with Broadway Show Gig," *ABC News*, August 1, 2015, http://bit.ly /MoteltoBroadway.

9   Tan.

15   Erin Bried, "Stretching Beauty: Ballerina Misty Copeland on Her Body Struggles," *Self*, March 17, 2014, http://bit.ly/bodystruggles.

17   Rebecca Gross, "Art Talk with Ballerina Misty Copeland," National Endowment for the Arts, June 8, 2011, https://www.arts.gov/art-works/2011/art-talk -ballerina-misty-copeland.

23   Michael Cooper, "Misty Copeland Is Promoted to Principal Dancer at American Ballet Theater," *New York Times*, June 30, 2015, http://bit.ly /principalballerina.

27   Moira Forbes, "Misty Copeland on Shattering Stereotypes and Redefining the Future of Ballet," *Forbes*, November 15, 2018, http://bit.ly /shatteringstereotypes.

LEARN MORE

American Ballet Theatre
https://www.abt.org/

Copeland, Misty. *Ballerina Body: Dancing and Eating Your Way to a Leaner, Stronger, and More Graceful You.* New York: Grand Central Life & Style, 2017.

———. *Firebird.* New York: G. P. Putnam's Sons, 2014.

———. *Life in Motion: An Unlikely Ballerina.* New York: Aladdin, 2016.

———. *Your Life in Motion: A Guided Journal for Discovering the Fire in You.* New York: Aladdin, 2018.

Metropolitan Opera
https://www.metopera.org/

Misty Copeland
https://mistycopeland.com/

Project Plié
https://www.abt.org/community/diversity-inclusion/project-plie/

INDEX

PHOTO ACKNOWLEDGMENTS

Image credits: Lillian Cunningham/The Washington Post/Getty Images, p. 4; Joe Sohm/Visions of America/Universal Images Group/Getty Images, p. 6; AFP/Getty Images, p. 7; Ken Wolter/Shutterstock.com, p. 8; DenisProduction.com/Shutterstock.com, p. 10; AP Photo/Kevin Karzin, pp. 11, 12; Matt Carasella/Patrick McMullan/Getty Images, p. 13; Gilbert Carrasquillo/FilmMagic/Getty Images, p. 15; Hiroyuki Ito/Getty Images, p. 16; AP Photo/Desmond Boylan/Pool, p. 17; Adam Bettcher//agency/Getty Images, p. 18; AP Photo/Diane Bondareff/Invision for Barbie, p. 19; AP Photo/Chris Dillmann/Vail Daily, p. 21; J. Countess/Getty Images, p. 22; Paras Griffin/2016 Essence Festival/Getty Images, p. 23; Bruce Glikas/FilmMagic/Getty Images, p. 24; Johnny Nunez/WireImage/Getty Images, p. 25; Mat Hayward/Getty Images, p. 26; Kris Connor/Getty Images, p. 27.

Cover: Mireya Acierto/Getty Images.